WHERE DID GRANDPA HIDE HIS MONEY?

Dedicated to my ever-enduring family.

PREFACE

Grandpa Otis belonged to the "the greatest generation" as defined by Tom Brokaw in his best selling book. He was an American citizen who came of age during the Great Depression and the Second World War and went on to build modern America.

He prided himself on work well done; loved baseball and his family and even went to church at Easter and Christmas. He also distrusted banks, thought most people in government were crooks and was genuinely afraid of Communists and hippies taking over the country.

He kept some savings in the bank, but recalling the Depression years and how his father lost all of his money when the bank shut its doors forever, he also hid money in places known only to him.

Some of it was buried in coffee cans in the garden. He was an avid gardener and he could keep an eye on it while tending his vegetables. A couple of jars filled with his poker night winnings were buried under the doghouse. His wife detested the mongrel that followed him home from work one day, but he got attached to him, called him "Killer," and watched in dismay as he barked at any passing stranger, but turned tail and ran from the neighbor's cat.

As he got older and was less and less able to work in his garden, Grandpa Otis began hiding money in places inside his home. He hid money in the freezer, in the pockets of old suits and coats, and even tucked a few bills inside the spine of the family Bible.

His wife passed when he was 70; he followed her just six months later. His children began the task of collecting; sorting and disposing of all of the possessions he had accumulated in his 74 years of life on this planet.

His oldest son kept the sack of marbles and a stack of baseball cards he had saved from his long ago youth. Another son took his medals from his Army service in the Second World War.

The daughters divided the dishes and knick-knacks. They cleaned out the freezer and threw away the countless Tupperware containers of what they thought were frozen vegetables. The rest, including the house and his 1970 cherry red Cadillac, went to the auction block. The money was undiscovered.

This story illustrates the common practices of generations of individuals who have hoarded and hidden money. They did so for a number of reasons-uncertain times due to economic collapse, wars and distrust of political and financial institutions, hope that a few dollars tucked away meant security in their old age and even illness.

Frequently, their families knew nothing of the money they secreted in places known only to them. They left no maps, no instructions with their wills (if they had one) and sometimes simply forgot with the passage of time where they hid their money.

If hidden money is found, it is often badly deteriorated because it had been secreted in places unfriendly to paper money and metal coins. Old money can look completely different from the currency of the current generation. The discoverer may have no clue as to the true value of what they've found.

This book will address some of these issues. My intent is not to make you an expert treasure hunter or coin collector. But you will gain some insights on why and where old money may be hidden, what to do with it when you find it and who can help you make the best decisions for preserving it or disposing of it. You already know persons who can advise you. Your banker is a good place to start. He or she probably knows reputable individuals that can consult with you on your discovery.

So sit back, enjoy the following pages and, when you've finished the book, think about talking to Grandma or Grandpa about hidden money or start looking for your own treasure. For lots of people, it's out there.

INTRODUCTION

Every year, our business, River City Coins, receives phone calls concerning old money turned into banks, or used to purchase groceries, pay the newspaper person, or even to make medical payments. We've also had people call us because they found a stash of old money in a home they recently purchased or they have a handful of old money discovered when Grandpa was moved to a care facility.

Much of this money comes from senior citizens that saved their coins and paper money at a time when they were worth only their face value.

Today, a silver dollar may be worth six dollars due to its silver content alone. Many senior citizens do not know this and spend a silver dollar thinking it is only worth one dollar.

Over the years, incredible hoards of old money have been discovered. In Iowa, one of the better-known incidents was the hoard of old coins found by a group of boys in Bayard, Iowa in the early 1960's.

More recently, hidden treasure was found in 1991 when a church excavated a piece of property for a parking lot in Selma, Iowa. There is a copy of the newspaper story regarding this hoard further along in the book. Unfortunately, many of the coins were in poor condition from being buried in the ground. The paper money was badly damaged. Some of it was unrecognizable.

The following pages are intended as a guide to the value of old money. I will also address the history of money in the United States, famous hoards and where old money may be hidden, preserving old money and where and how to sell it if you should be lucky enough to have it or find it.

Most importantly, this book is a wake-up call for senior citizens who may have hidden old money and do not fully understand its true value and the importance of making sure it's not hidden so well that it may become lost and irretrievable.

CHAPTER ONE

WHAT'S IT WORTH?

There are many factors that determine the value of old coins and paper money. These include:

1. **Condition.** Obviously, coins that are undamaged and have not been cleaned are going to be worth more than coins that are corroded or have surface scratches or flaws or have been aggressively cleaned.

Coin dealers and collectors will often talk about a coins "grade". Grading is a universal system used to evaluate coins.

The following show the different grades for a Mercury Dime:

Uncirculated

Extra Fine

Very Fine

Fine

Very Good

Good

About Good

Grading is used only for collectible coins; not coins that are considered to be worth only their silver content. Thus, a handful of circulated, worn 1950's Washington silver quarters will be evaluated for their silver content, only. A dealer will count them up and make you an offer. He will not take the time to grade them and appraise each coin because they are not rare and not collectible in low grades (unless someone is trying to build a set of each year and mint mark).

A 1932S Washington Quarter is a different story. Because it is rare (only 408,000 were originally made verses a 1952 quarter with a mintage of 38,862,073) and highly sought after by collectors, it will be graded and priced accordingly.

Unless you want to become a coin collector, it isn't necessary to learn grading. But you will understand why a dealer may select certain coins and scrutinize them more carefully while other coins may be put in a pile and priced according to their precious metals content, only.

2. **Rarity.** There are many reasons why coins can be rare. Some coins are rare because so few of them become available in the market. Others are rare because the U.S. Mint made so few of them in a particular year.

As an example, most Washington Quarters are easy to obtain. They were first made in 1932. The silver ones (from 1932 to 1964) are generally worth 75 cents to $1.00 in average circulated condition because of their silver content, alone.

However, in each year, coins may have been made at one or more of the U.S. Mints (coin producing facilities). In 1932, Washington Quarters were made at all three mints. The Philadelphia Mint produced 5,404,000 quarters; the mint in Denver only produced 436,800 quarters and the mint in San Francisco made 408,000 quarters.

Consequently, a 1932 Washington Quarter from the Philadelphia Mint in fine condition is worth about $5.00. The same quarter minted in Denver is worth about $48.00 and the one minted in San Francisco is worth around $42.00.

Why? Many more of the '32 Philly quarters survived. The others are scarcer because fewer were made and over the years, because so many were lost or melted down for their silver content, they have become increasingly harder to find.

How do I know where my coin came from? I'll talk about that in a later chapter!

3. **Desirability.** Oh, you sexy thing!

Not all old paper money or coins are valuable just because they're old!

Over the centuries, all kinds of money were produced-everything from cowry shells to copper plates to actual hard currency.

In the United States, because so many people of different nationalities came here, it's not unusual to find money from other countries. Some of it is quite old.

However, if there are few collectors of that particular currency, it may have very little value. Also, there may be an abundant supply with more being discovered every day.

A good example is ancient Roman coins. Hoards of ancient Roman coins have been uncovered in archaeological digs, during modern excavations (subway tunnels, foundations for new buildings,

etc.) and by individuals that are plowing a field or digging a new well.

The coins they find may be thousands of years old. But, because so many have been found and can be easily purchased from a variety of sources, they may be worth only one to five dollars individually.

Collectors may find some series of coins and paper money particularly attractive and desirable.

Right now, old U.S. paper money is "hot"!

Large size U.S. bank notes (see Chapter 4.) and Nationals (large and small size bank notes) are in demand, in any condition. Presently, a Large Size 1923 $1.00 Silver Certificate in fine condition is worth around $40-$60.

Example of a National Currency Note:

4. **Promotion.** Some coins may artificially be worth more than others simply because they're being "hyped" or promoted by special interest groups.

   An investment fund may tell you in their literature that now is the time to buy U.S. gold or that silver dollars are only available in limited numbers. The TV Shopping channels will offer once in a lifetime opportunities to buy certain coins.

   Coin dealers may recommend certain issues, not because they are especially rare or valuable in a particular grade, but because they have an oversupply of that particular coin.

Caveat Emptor: Let the Buyer Beware certainly applies here!!

The best advice one can offer is to learn as much as you can by reading about coins that interest you or do comparison-shopping. If someone is talking you into investing in bullion or rare coins, do the research. There is plenty of free information out there on precious metals, market trends and performances.

It's impossible to tell you in this book what every coin or piece of paper money you may run into is worth. There are a number of ways, though, that you can determine if something may have value or not. There are hundreds of web sites that feature old money. Public libraries are a good source of information, too.

You can also have your coins or paper money appraised by a professional. Most will charge a fee for this service. Always try to get two appraisals, especially if you have a large collection or many older coins with pre-1900 dates.

The following may be helpful:

<u>ITEMS OF LITTLE VALUE OR "FACE" VALUE ONLY</u>

1. Susan B. Anthony dollars and Sacagawea gold dollars have no silver content and are very common. They are worth only one dollar.

2. Kennedy half-dollars dated 1971 to now are only worth 50 cents. They are not scarce and have no silver content.

3. "Drummer Boy" Quarters are worth 25 cents; they, too, are very common.

4. Bicentennial $2.00 notes are presently worth only their face value. They are not rare.

5. Most 1930's to 1950's wheat pennies are very common. Pre-1935 wheat pennies should be checked for special dates and mint marks. A 1914D cent in Good condition may be an $85.00 coin; a 1931S is worth $34.00 in Good condition.

6. Foreign coins and paper notes-after 1900-have little or no collector interest or value.

ITEMS OF VALUE

1. Half dollars, quarters and dimes minted in 1964 and before have a composition of .900 silver and .100 copper. If they are not rare or collectible, they still have value because of their silver content.

   How much they are worth is tied directly to the value of an ounce of silver. The current value can be found in many newspapers, or on line, as the "Spot" price of silver or any broker can tell you what it is.

One-dollar face value in dimes, quarters or halves contains about .712 oz of pure silver.

To determine the value of a half dollar, you take the price of an ounce of silver, say, $13.00 and multiply it times .712 times .50. Your silver half dollar is worth $4.62.

A dealer or bullion buyer may offer less so he can make a profit.

2. U.S. Silver Dollars. Beginning in 1878 the US government began making the "Liberty Head" Silver dollar. Later it became known as the "Morgan" silver dollar named after the designer George T. Morgan. In 1904 production of all silver dollars stopped, then resumed again in 1921.

Obverse of 1880 American Morgan Type Silver Dollar

Reverse of 1881-S American Morgan Type Silver Dollar

In 1921 the US government made what became known as the "peace" silver dollar, celebrating the end of World War I. In 1935 production of all silver dollars stopped for several decades.

Peace Dollar, 1921-1935

Starting in 1986, the United States Mint began making American Eagle Silver Dollar coins. These are produced each year. Considered by many to be one of the most beautiful American coin designs. It is modeled after the old Walking Liberty half-dollars. Each official US dollar coin contains one ounce of pure silver.

New Silver Eagle

Silver dollars or "cartwheels," contain .77344 ounces of pure silver. A common date silver dollar is worth about $10 to $18 depending on condition and the silver market. Scarcer dates can be worth much more. It's important to know what dates are rare.

3. Kennedy half-dollars from 1965-1970 are 40% silver. 1964 Kennedy half-dollars are 90% silver.

4. U.S. Large Size paper money has value in most any condition. I will discuss paper money in another chapter. Large Size U.S. bank notes were made from 1861-1929. Small size notes were made from 1929 to now.

5. Small size U.S. currency is becoming increasingly collectible and should be appraised. Collectors prefer notes in about unused or new condition. A 1957 Series $1.00 Silver Certificate is worth just .15 to .25 more than the face value, if the note is worn and has been heavily circulated. A new note may be worth 3 to 4 times the face value.

6. "Good For" store trade tokens with town names and businesses on them, prison tokens, Civilian Conservation Corps and military tokens are widely collected. Some can be very valuable.

Eddyville, Iowa G.E.
Stephenson Druggist Token

CCC TOKEN

EXAMPLE OF A MILITARY TOKEN

Tax tokens, transportation tokens, OPA tokens, etc. are seldom collected and consequently are not valuable.

7. Souvenir sets, mint sets and proof sets should be kept in their original packaging. If the coins have darkened, do not remove them from their packages and try to clean them.

8. Worlds Fair Coins, Tokens and Medallions are highly sought after.

9. Jewelry made from old coins is very collectible. "Love tokens" are coins with one side polished down smooth with an inscription and/or design. Some can be quite elaborate. Typically, they were

worn as pins or on a necklace. I have had a gold coin that was made into a Love Token.

BARBER COIN MADE INTO A LOVE TOKEN

10. Gold coins and medals. I will talk more about

U.S. gold coins in a later chapter.

11. Pre-140 Bank Checks with nice vignettes, stock certificates, bonds and even credit cards are other items of interest to collectors.

12. Punchboards are growing in popularity as a collectible, too. The term "punchboard" (or in some cases "punch board", "push board", "punch card", or "push card") refers to a gambling device popular in the United States from roughly 1900 until 1970.

Typical Push card

BIG GRID GAME WINNERS PUNCHBOARD

Punchboards were particularly popular during the 1930's, 1940's and 1950's. Although they are illegal to operate in many states, you can still find punchboards being played today in some areas of the country, particularly as fund-raisers for clubs and organizations. Ones that are risqué or have patriotic themes, comic book characters or advertise a well-known product are especially sought after.

It's impossible to make a complete list of everything that relates to coins and paper money and may be valuable. When it doubt, ask. Or try to find a similar item in reference books or on line web sites.

CHAPTER TWO

WHAT THE HECK IS THIS?

Most of us are familiar with what a penny, nickel, dime and so forth look like. How about a Three-Cent Silver or a Trade Dollar?

Over the years, the mints have produced denominations of coins that certainly get peoples

attention. Odd denomination coins, such as the three cent pieces, are thought to be foreign coins and of little value. In fact, twenty cent pieces, half cents and so on are more valuable than many familiar U.S. coins because they were minted for only short periods of time and the number of surviving specimens is usually very small.

The following chart presents all regular U.S. issues from the very first coins minted:

History of Regular Issue United States Coin Denominations

(Denominations in Bold Type Are Still Authorized)

HALF CENT	1793-1857
CENT	**1793 TO DATE**
TWO CENT PIECE	1864-1873
SILVER THREE-CENT PIECE	1851-1873
NICKEL THREE-CENT PIECE	1865-1889

NICKEL FIVE-CENT PIECE	**1866 TO DATE**
HALF DIME	1794-1873
DIME	**1796 TO DATE**
TWENTY-CENT PIECE	1875-1878

QUARTER DOLLAR	**1796 TO DATE**
HALF DOLLAR	**1794 TO DATE**

DOLLAR   **1794 TO DATE**
(Includes Eisenhower:
1971-1978 and Susan
B. Anthony: 1979 to
1981.)

Note: This list does not include regular issue gold coins.

Any good coin reference book will have illustrations of these coins. The following are illustrations of some of the odd denomination coins you may encounter:

**HALF-CENT PIECES, MINTED FROM 1793-1857.
CENTS.**

TWO-CENT PIECES, MINTED 1864-1873

**THREE CENT SILVER PIECES, MINTED 1865-1873
(ALSO KNOWN AS "TRIMES")**

A NICKEL 3-CENT PIECE WAS ALSO MADE FROM 1863 TO 1869. IT HAS A DIFFERENT APPEARANCE (SEE BELOW).

1869 THREE CENT NICKEL

TWENTY-CENT PIECES, MINTED 1875-1878

CHAPTER THREE

U.S. GOLD COINS

The U.S issued gold coins for general circulation from about 1838 to 1933. The design for gold coins was altered in 1907 from the Liberty Head designs used until then to the Indian Head and Saint-Gaudens motifs. These coins remained in circulation until the Great Depression

in 1933 when most gold coins then in circulation were recalled by the U. S. mint and melted down. Many gold coins therefore disappeared contributing to their rarity today.

Many people have at least one or more gold coins in their possession. Few people, however, are aware of the actual gold content of such coins or of their current numismatic values.

The following provides information on the gold content of the most popular U.S. gold coins and a rough estimate of the current numismatic values for such coins based on a coin graded XF (Extra Fine).

(This was written when an ounce of gold was $660.00. The price of gold factors into the value.)

$1 Gold Liberty Head (1849-1854)
Weight: .0538 troy oz.
Fineness: .900 or 21.6 karats
Diameter: 13mm
Fine Gold Content: .0483 troy oz.
Estimated Value: $165

$1 Gold Indian Princess (1854-1856) Weight:
.0538 troy oz.
Fineness: .900 or 21.6 karats
Diameter: 15mm
Fine Gold Content: .0483 troy oz.
Estimated Value: $340

$1 Gold Indian Head (1856-1889)
Weight: .0538 troy oz.
Fineness: .900 or 21.6 karats
Diameter: 15mm
Fine Gold Content: .0483 troy oz.
Estimated Value: $170

$2 1/2 Liberty Quarter Eagle (1840-1907)
Weight: .1343 troy oz.
Fineness: .900 or 21.6 karats
Diameter: 17mm

Fine Gold Content: .1209 troy oz.
Estimated Value: $185

$5 Liberty Half Eagle (1866-1908)
Weight: .26875 troy oz.
Fineness: .900 or 21.6 karats
Diameter: 21mm
Fine Gold Content: .2419 troy oz.
Estimated Value: $180

$5 Indian Half Eagle (1908-1929)
Weight: .26875 troy oz.
Fineness: .900 or 21.6 karats
Diameter: 21mm
Fine Gold Content: .2419 troy oz.
Estimated Value: $255

$10 Liberty Eagle (1866-1907)
Weight: .5375 troy oz.
Fineness: .900 or 21.6 karats
Diameter: 27mm
Fine Gold Content: .4838 troy oz.
Estimated Value: $315

$10 Indian Eagle (1907-1933)
Weight: .5375 troy oz.
Fineness: .900 or 21.6 karats
Diameter: 27mm

Fine Gold Content: .4838 troy oz.
Estimated Value: $365

$20 Liberty Double Eagle (1877-1907)
Weight: 1.0750 troy oz.

Fineness: .900 or 21.6 karats
Diameter: 34mm
Fine Gold Content: .9675 troy oz.
Estimated Value: $650

$20 St. Gaudens Double Eagle (1907-1933)
Weight: 1.0750 troy oz.
Fineness: .900 or 21.6 karats
Diameter: 34mm
Fine Gold Content: .9675 troy oz.
Estimated Value: $670

The following shows the differences in the Liberty Head design vs. the St. Gaudens design for a $20 Gold Piece:

US $20.00 LIBERTY (COMMONLY CALLED A DOUBLE EAGLE IN THIS DENOMINATION)

$20 ST. GAUDENS DOUBLE EAGLE, NAMED FOR THE DESIGNER, AUGUSTUS ST. GAUDENS

A $3.00 gold piece was also minted from 1854 to 1889. It is 20.5 millimeters in size and contains 0.1452 ounces of gold. Mintages for each year were very small. Consequently, it is a rarely encountered gold piece with prices starting at $400. in Fine condition.

CHAPTER FOUR

U.S. PAPER MONEY

When Congress authorized the first paper money (properly called "demand notes") on July 17, 1861, it brought an end to a turbulent era of private banks, obsolete or broken bank notes (notes issued by banks that went "bust") and banking instability. For the first time, the U.S. government took over the proper printing and distribution of paper money. The Secretary of the Treasury and the Office of the Treasurer of the United States became the vehicle for all financial and monetary functions of the federal government.

In the decades that followed, U.S. paper money went through a variety of note types (depending in large part on how they were guaranteed or redeemable), with the notes from the National Banking periods being some of the most valuable and collected. These notes were issued from the time of the Civil War to about 1935, when the Federal Reserve Banking System came into being.

Notes during the National Bank Notes period have an assigned charter number and the name and the location of the represented bank on the note.

In my home state of Iowa, Burlington, Iowa had four banks that issued "Nationals" with the bank name on them. Smaller towns in the area, such as New London and Mount Pleasant, also had banks with "Nationals;" these notes are quite valuable because fewer were issued and not many survived. Altogether, Iowa had 542 banks that issued National Bank Notes through 1935.

Bank notes from the time of the Civil War to 1928 were large in size and sometimes referred to as "horse blankets".

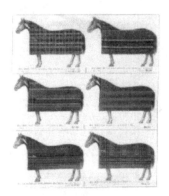

1891 $1 Large Size Silver Certificate

In 1929 standardized currency was introduced. U.S. notes were reduced in size by 25 percent and standardized with uniform portraits on the faces and emblems and monuments on the backs.

Today, more than 99 percent of the total dollar amount of paper money in circulation in the United States is made up of Federal Reserve notes. The other small part of circulating currency consists of U.S. notes or legal tender notes still in circulation but no longer issued.

Federal Reserve notes are printed and issued in denominations of $1, $2, $5, $10, $20, $50, and $100. The $500, $1,000, $5,000, and $10,000 denominations have not been printed since 1946.

The Federal Reserve Act requires that adequate backing be pledged for all Federal Reserve notes in circulation. U.S. Treasury securities, acquired through open market operations, are the most important form of collateral and provide backing for most of the value of the currency in circulation. Some other types of collateral the Federal Reserve holds are gold certificates and certain eligible instruments such as notes, drafts, and bills of exchange. The Federal Reserve System established by Congress in 1913, issues Federal Reserve notes through its 12 Federal Reserve Districts. Every district has its main office in a major city, and all but two

have branches in other large cities. A number and the corresponding letter of the alphabet designate each district.

The Bureau of Engraving and Printing, a division of the U.S. Treasury Department, produces currency for the Federal Reserve System to replace damaged or worn notes or to support

economic growth. Federal Reserve Banks issue currency according to the need in their districts. The district letter and number on the face of a note identify the issuing Reserve Bank.

Federal Reserve Banks are located in the following 12 cities:

CITY	LETTER	NUMBER
Boston	A	1
New York	B	2
Philadelphia	C	3
Cleveland	D	4
Richmond	E	5
Atlanta	F	6
Chicago	G	7

St. Louis	H	8
Minneapolis	I	9
Kansas City	J	10
Dallas	K	11
San Francisco	L	12

Today, paper money is "RED HOT!" and the demand for notes in nice condition far exceeds the supply.

If you discover old paper money, always have it looked at before you turn it in to a bank. $500. and

$1,000. notes still show up from time to time. They are legal to own and collectors pay a premium for them. But once the bank takes them in, they cannot be reissued. So, if you find one, it's best to locate a buyer rather than take it to a bank.

Paper money may be graded like coins. Some notes, because of their rarity, are valuable in any condition. More common notes, like silver certificates from the 1930's and 1950's, are only valuable in new or uncirculated condition. A 1957 One Dollar silver certificate that shows a lot of wear may be worth only 15 cents to 20 cents over its face value; the same note in new condition may be worth $1 to $3 over face.

The following illustrates a few U.S. bank notes collected today:

1928 $1 Silver Certificate "Funnyback" (the back is different from other $1 notes)

1928 D Series Red Seal $2 Legal Tender Note

1928 E Series Red Seal $5.00 Note

Example of a National Bank Note. The note has the name of the bank, town and state on the note, along with its assigned charter number (1301).

Because of the danger of a Japanese invasion of
Hawaii in 1942, specially marked United States
money was substituted for normal notes. These

notes had brown serial numbers and treasury seal, and were overprinted on the back on the note with the word "Hawaii."

The $1 Hawaii notes have the series date 1935A and are worth $3 to $8. $5 Hawaii notes were issued with the 1934 and 1934A series date and these are worth $8 to $15. The $10 Hawaii note was issued with the series date 1934A and is worth $15 to $20 in average condition.

If you want to learn more about paper money, most libraries have books about U.S. currency and its history. There are also countless sites on the

Internet, including the web pages of clubs and professional organizations, such as the Society of Paper Money Collectors, Inc.

The following is an interesting story from The Boston Globe:

The Boston Globe
Pair digs up buried hoard in Methuen

By David Abel, Globe Staff | April 26, 2005

It's everyone's fantasy, a dream we always wake up from, tormented that the images of our sleep are just illusions. That is, finding buried treasure.

One morning three weeks ago, such a fairy tale suddenly came true for Barry Villcliff and Tim Crebase, two friends trying to dig up a small tree in Crebase's yard in Methuen, they said.

Using a spade to get at the roots, Crebase heard a thud, and about a foot down, he saw he had hit a piece of wood. The 23-year-old roofer then realized the wood was part a 2-foot-wide box.

He kept digging until he ripped the top off and found nine rusted tin cans, which decades ago -- maybe nearly a century ago -- held ginger cookies and dough. Crebase wrapped the cans in a sweatshirt and carried them to a nearby truck, where he and

Villcliff, his 27-year-old boss from Manchester, N.H., began cracking them open.

"It didn't look like anything we ever saw before," Villcliff said in a phone interview last night. Then he caught a glimpse of Crebase's face and knew he found something valuable.

"I'm a pessimist; I was waiting until I got a professional review before I jumped to any conclusions," Villcliff said. "Tim, however, was singing and dancing. He was ranting like a rabid monkey."

When they finished emptying the old cans in a milk crate, they saw before them about 1,800 bills -- including more than 900 $1 bills, 200 $2 bills, and 300 $20 bills dated from 1899 to 1929, they said. There were also a pile of gold and silver certificates and scores of notes from local banks in Methuen, Haverhill, Amesbury, Newburyport, and beyond.

The two went back to work, but later that afternoon made their way to the Village Coin Shop in Plaistow, N.H. When they walked in with their milk crate full of old greenbacks, Domenic Mangano, the shop's owner, quickly locked the door behind them.

"I was thinking, 'I've never seen anything like this in my life,' " said Mangano, who estimates their find is worth more than $100,000.

He knew they were genuine, he said, because fake bills look purposely aged.

None of the men know why the money was hidden in Crebase's yard, but they have their theories.

One is that the stash was the proceeds of a robbery. Another is that it was profits hoarded from bootlegging during Prohibition. Or, they figure, it could be the savings of immigrants who didn't trust the local banks.

Long-lost buried bills may be worth more than $100,000.

CHAPTER FIVE

HIDDEN MONEY

Ever since Adam and Eve, people have hidden money and valuables (Adam didn't have to eat the apple Eve offered him; he had already buried a bushel).

People hide money for a variety of reasons-global instability, distrust of banks, habits learned from parents and grandparents, compulsive behavior and a lot of other reasons. All too often, though, the person who hides money forgets where they hid it, becomes mentally incapacitated or dies.

Plenty has been told about lost pirate treasures, stolen money that was never recovered, etc. What I'm talking about is something more mundane but equally fascinating.

I've already mentioned a couple of instances where old money was rediscovered long after the person who hid it lost it or died. Since we opened our coin business in 1989, we have personally been involved in or heard of instances where old money was rediscovered.

Among my favorites are:

1. In 1991, a lady in a small town in Illinois was cleaning her garage for a yard sale her daughter wanted to have. She came across a small suitcase in a corner of the garage.

When she tried to pick it up, it was so heavy she couldn't lift it. It was locked and she didn't have a key.

Her son-in-law pried it open with a crow bar. Inside were sixty rolls of U.S. silver dollars (the final count was 1,197 coins). Her bank contacted me. I appraised the coins at a little over $10,000. She had no idea where they came from; her husband had been deceased for quite awhile.

She decided not to sell them at the time. I have no idea what finally became of them.

2. A lady from Dallas City, Illinois was out digging berry bushes. She came across about $200. in old coins in an old coffee can. She brought the can to our shop. She said someone had recently

dumped a bunch of household stuff in the ravine. The can wasn't rusted, which indicated to me this had happened recently.

The coins were worth around $550.00.

3. We were asked to look at some coins recovered after a trailer fire. The owner had died some time ago and the trailer was unoccupied.

The coins were at a bank. There were very few single coins; most were fused into lumps of silver that showed partial dates, etc. As I recall, there was approximately 6 to 10 pounds of melted coins.

I gave the bank the name of a refinery that would buy the "lumps" for their silver value.

More silver coins were found when the trailer site was cleaned up. I purchased around sixty half dollars that were scorched but not melted or disfigured by the fire.

4. I met a gentleman who told me he collected coins. He was looking for some special dates. I had the opportunity to help him acquire the coins he wanted and later appraised his collection for him. He had a large quantity of silver coins; most

of it was fairly common but there were a few
better date silver dollars.

He called me twice after I saw them and
suggested he might want to sell them, but he
never did.

About a year after I last spoke to him, his son

contacted me. His father had died and he found
my business card in his home. He knew his
father had a large coin collection and that he
never sold it. The problem was nobody could
find it.

I recalled that the coins were in musty smelling
milk cartons and metal ammo boxes. I suggested
they might be hidden somewhere on his property.

They searched the trailer and property; they even
pulled the siding off of the trailer. They never
found the coins and I believe they are still there.

My appraisal in 1995 indicates I valued them at $12,000.

5. I enjoy auctions. I attended one in Burlington, Iowa about two years ago that had a large quantity of "junk silver". The silver money was found in two garbage cans in the garage. According to the owner's son, he didn't know the coins were there and the garage was never locked.

I have also bought books at auction and found money hidden in them. Money is sometimes found at auctions in old clothes and appliances, too.

6. A man from Ft. Madison, Iowa discovered a small cache of old silver coins in the stairs of a house he was demolishing. Some of the coins dated to the mid-1800's.

7. A couple found about $600. in paper money under some area rugs in a home they inherited. Their first impulse was to take it to the bank and deposit it. Fortunately, they contacted me before doing that.

The majority of the notes were 1930's series silver certificates in new condition, worth 2 to 5 times their face value.

A person with Alzheimer's may hide or hoard things. The following is an example of what to do from "Alzheimer's Resources for Caregivers":

"What are some tips for dealing with an Alzheimer's patient who rummages around or hides things?

Caring for a patient who rummages around or hides things in the home is a challenge, but not an insurmountable one. Try some of the following ideas.

- Lock certain rooms or cabinets to protect their contents; lock up all valuables.
- Remove or prevent access to unsafe substances, such as cleaning products, alcohol, and medications. Patients with dementia sometimes overdose on alcohol.

- Prevent electrical accidents by blocking unused electrical outlets with childproofing devices.
- Designate a special drawer of items that the person can "play" with when they are bored.
- Arrange for your mail to be delivered to a post office box or out of reach of the Alzheimer's patient.

- Restrict access to wastebaskets and trashcans. Check all wastebaskets before disposing of their contents, in case objects have been hidden there.
- Learn the person's preferred hiding places and look there first to find hidden objects."

Favorite hiding places include:

1. Old books
2. Tops of curtains
3. Freezers
4. Buried money (usually hidden in easy view of a window or door).
5. Out buildings (chicken houses were favorite places because chickens are a natural alarm system).

6. Overcoats, dresses and suit pockets

Other hiding places we have had experience with:

1. A coin slot carved into a kitchen wall. The space behind the wall was filled with coins of all denominations.
2. Behind a bar back. Tradition had it that the saloonkeeper would toss coins up and behind the back of his bar. Sure enough, when the bar was closed and dismantled, a large quantity of coins (mostly pennies and nickels, dating from the 1920's forward) was found behind the bar back.

3. A false bottom inside a bathroom vanity. Jars of coins were discovered under the false bottom; it had two finger holes for easy removal.

A similar setup was found under the kitchen sink.

4. The cavity under a doorsill. The doorsill was nailed down; the hiding place was discovered when the house was demolished. Half a dozen Indian cents and a row of empty baby food jars indicated it was once used to hide money.
5. The ductwork in a house. This has been reported more than once.

One person told us they found coffee cans filled with silver coins hidden inside a furnace pipe. Another told us they found jars of old money on top of the ductwork.

6. Inside wells and cisterns.

It is very important that if you are the one hiding old money that you leave a map and clear instructions as to its location. I would recommend that copies be included with your will, in your safety deposit box and in a large, clearly labeled envelope in a dresser drawer.

It is equally important that you hide your money in a place where insects, moisture, heat, etc will not damage

it. I will offer some tips for preserving old money in the next chapter.

The following articles are a sampling of hoards lost and found and others still awaiting discovery:

One of my favorite websites is: www.losttreasure usa.com/StateTreasures/StateTreasures.htm.

The site features great stories about lost treasure by state. I have selected Illinois, Iowa and Missouri. If you live in another state, please go to the web site for your location.

1. A cache of gold and silver coins is buried in an orchard on the old Taylor farm 5 miles north of Charleston.

2. Treasure is believed buried on the old Orville Lowery farm, about 2 miles S.W. of Helm.

   Numerous carvings of Indian or Spanish origin were found in 1925 and can still be seen.

3. A cache of treasure is supposedly located on the old Ferkle farm near what is now 34th Avenue and 14th Street in Rock Island.

4. After high waters recede each spring, silver dollars dated in the late 1800s are found along the west bank of the Ohio River near Golconda. The coins have been washed ashore for many years and local

stories say that they come from a wrecked steamboat that was carrying millions in silver.

5. A man named Shaffer owned an 80-acre farm 4 miles from Carlinville in the late 1800s and converted all of his profits into gold coins. After his death in the early 1900s, searches were made

for his buried coins but nothing was ever reported found.

6. During the 1920s prohibition, the Roger Touhy gang buried an estimated $60,000 in the area of Rockford. The cache went unrecovered when most of the gang was captured and sentenced to long prison terms.

7. In 1931 Harvey J. Bailey and his gang robbed a Lincoln, Neb. bank of over $1 million. He was sent to prison, for life, in 1933 and refused to tell where his main cache was. One of his hoards is

buried on a farm near Richmond, just below the Wisconsin state line.

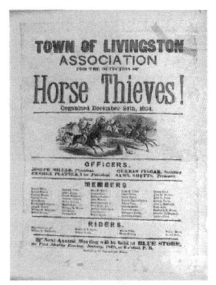

8. In the early 1800s, horse thieves operated in the area of Sabula, Iowa, and are believed to have buried money and loot across the river just south of Savanna. Lawmen chased the gang out of the

area and they never had time to recover their caches.

9. In the 1870s, Benjamin Boyd and Dr. Briggs were successful counterfeiters, passing bogus cash all over the state of Illinois. They used the Abbott farm near Unionville as a headquarters until 1875

when U.S. government agents caught up with them and sent the pair to prison. When the old Abbott farmhouse was moved across the road to its present location, several bundles of bogus bills and

the engraved plates were found in the basement. Local stories say that several caches of legitimate currency and gold coins remain hidden somewhere on the old farm site.

10.   David and Taylor Driscoll led a gang of outlaws in the 1830s. In 1841, the gang was captured and shot, but the Driscolls escaped and were never seen again. It is believed that several caches from their robberies and stagecoach

holdups remain buried near their hiding place on a farm south of DeKalb, one reported cache amounts to $30,000.

1. A band of Indians robbed an army payroll wagon around 1842. An old Indian said the gold coins were buried along Miner's Creek near Guttenburg.

2. A wealthy lumberman filled an iron cooking pot

with stocks, bonds and gold coins and buried it near the banks of the Mississippi River at a place now known as River Front Park in Clinton.

3. There are stories that buried treasure is associated with Cold Water Cave, located about 25 miles from Decorah, on the (1935) farm of a man named Gaul.

4. Numerous treasure caches are reportedly buried in Stone Park and in the hills overlooking the bend in the Missouri River at Sioux City.

5. Between $35,000-$50,000 in gold was stolen during a train robbery along the Mississippi River west of Davenport at Buffalo.

The loot is believed to be buried in a 3-acre area just off the railroad tracks and highway near the creek in the area.

In the 1800s, Red Brussels lived in a log cabin on an island in Trumbull Lake near Terril. A group of irate vigilantes tracked some stolen horses to his place and hung him. Brussel's cache of money and valuables is still believed to remain there.

6. Around 1863, there was a grove of trees about 1/2 mile southeast of Harcourt on the Orville Anderson farm. An outlaw buried his loot there.

7. A gang of outlaws and cattle rustlers, known as the Banditti of the Plains, headquartered near the mouth of the Boone River in the 1800s. It is believed that they buried their loot in an ancient Indian mound located in the immediate area and never recovered the cache. The mound is covered by a thick growth of oak trees and is located near the John Lott Monument.

8. Soldier of fortune Thomas Nelson came to Cerro Gordo County and took a job at the Wheeler

Ranch in 1884. He brought with him a large quantity of gold coins and word soon spread of his wealth. Fearing that he would be robbed, he buried

the hoard somewhere on the Winnebago River between the Wheeler Ranch and the Horseshoe Bend area in a 3-foot deep hole. He was never able to locate the exact spot again.

9. In 1893, farmer John W. (last name unknown) buried $50,000 in gold coins in casks on his property, 4 miles from Eldora. He went insane in 1897 and cold not remember where his treasure was buried. It was never recovered.

1. Ellis Trast buried a cache of stolen outlaw loot about 3 miles outside of Huzzah. The cache was carried up a small hollow from Haunted Springs to a shelter rock and put in a foxhole under a bluff and covered with rocks. The  skull of a horse head was left as a marker.

2. There are legends that tell of a cache of Spanish

treasure buried in the area of Noble Hill, on Hwy 13, about 13 miles north of Springfield on the Polk-Greene County line.

3. The outlaw Hillary Farrington buried a cache of loot on the old Duram farm at Jeona.

4. A cache of gold coins known as the Kaffer Treasure is buried in the area of Armstrong.

5. Around 1927, $25,000 in gems and jewelry, hidden by bandits who robbed a jewelry store, was buried at the foot of an old oak tree between two large roots about 6 miles east of Independence.

True Tales of Hidden Treasure

Did you ever read a story — fiction, of course — of a great treasure find? Many novels and myths contain such adventures and discoveries. In reality, real treasures of coins, currency, gold and jewels have been found.

The famous King Tut tomb, with its treasures and mummy of the pharaoh, created a worldwide sensation in the 1920s. The treasures are on tour for the second time.

More recent treasure hoards and lesser finds still make the news from time to time. In 1974, the estate of eccentric recluse LaVere Redfield of

Carson City was taken over by the state when he died. In examining his ramshackle home, they discovered a false wall with more than 400,000 silver dollars, mostly in mint condition, stashed in bags behind it. At a court-ordered auction in 1976 the hoard was sold to the highest bidder for more than $7 million. Today many of these "Redfield" dollars are trading at hundreds of dollars each, with a gross value well in excess of $100 million.

In 1985 the group known as Treasure Salvors, diving off the coast of Florida, came across the

treasure of a sunken Spanish ship,
the Atocha. This find eventually had to be
divided between the state of Florida and other
claimants, and when tallied, the proceeds
exceeded $20 million. Most of recovered treasure
was gold coins and ingots. The site was scoured
for many years thereafter.

Around 1950 an old building in rural Georgia
was being demolished when, in the rubble, a few

wooden kegs  were found
containing virtually mint-condition large cents,
all dated 1818. This "Randall hoard" eventually
was sold to dealers and collectors through
various public sales and eventually brought well
over $5 million.

A much more recent find made the news, as
well. Two men claimed to have found a hoard of
old currency in the 1870-1920 range in a can

buried on their land. As the story broke, it was shown that in fact, they found it in the loft of another man's barn.

The 1,800-plus banknotes were shown to a coin dealer in rural New Hampshire who put a rough figure of $125,000 on the hoard. Closer examination of the notes — most were in "very fine" condition — puts the value well over $1 million. Ownership is to be determined and the hoard will no doubt wind up in a major auction, eventually.

At an auction held by Mike Aron Rare Coins a few years ago, a group of very scarce 1860-O mint silver dollars was offered for sale. Each coin was coated with a grayish oxidation that gave the hoard the name, the "Chimney Hoard."

These coins were stored in the chimney of a home in the South during the Civil War and found 130 years later. The heat and soot

coated each coin with a grayish layer. They sold for $300 and up.

Perhaps the best hoard story is the one by our own Treasury Department. Since the closure of the New Orleans Mint in 1909 and the discontinuation of silver dollar production in 1935, bags of silver dollars (1,000 per bag) were shipped to Washington to be stored in the basement vaults of the Treasury building. In 1967 the Treasury decided to sell these bags at face value for cash, only to customers who came to the Treasury building on a designated day. The

three million or so silver dollars were sold within a few days. The coins varied from the very common 1922 Peace dollars to the very scarce 1859-O Seated Liberty dollars and rare Carson City (CC) dollars.

The U.S. Mint Carson City, Nevada

Then the General Services Administration decided the giveaway was not a great idea and began to sort through the remainders and insert them in hard plastic holders with the date and notation that they were from the U.S. Treasury hoard.

These coins, known as "GSA" dollars, were sold by mail and ranged from $15 to $350 each. Today, the common-date "CC" dollars sell for about $175 each. The scarcer dates, such as 1879-CC, sell for more than $4,000.

GSA DOLLAR IN PLASTIC

Chances are, if you can buy a 100- or 200-year-old house, there may be hidden treasure inside or even outside the home. Happy hunting.

The following article is about a treasure hoard that was found in Selma, Iowa. The coins and paper money had been buried so long that they were in very poor condition. Some of the paper money was unrecognizable.

HEIRS AWARDED BURIED TREASURE FROM THE 1930s

By Frank Santiago, The Des Moines Register, March 21, 1991

Charles Nelson, a blacksmith and carpenter in Selma, didn't trust banks during the Depression so he

buried his cash in tin cans and glass jars under the floor of his garage.

The hiding place, Nelson felt, was as safe as Fort Knox because he seldom left the property and, for insurance, parked his car over the spot and took out the

 key.

But Nelson didn't talk much about his hidden treasure, and the money was forgotten after he died. His daughter, Opal, died in 1981.

Wednesday, in an unusual case, the Iowa Supreme Court ruled that the treasure, with a face value of $25,000, belongs to Nelson's heirs, not the Selma United Methodist Church, which bought the old Nelson property. The church discovered the money when it cleared the land for a parking lot.

"Although the real estate was abandoned by Opal's estate, we believe that it would be completely unwarranted inference to conclude that the money found by the church had been abandoned by its owner," said the court.

Ottumwa lawyer H. Edwin Detlie, who represented the family, said the ruling is the first of its kind in the state dealing with ownership of lost or mislaid property.

Records show the Nelson home was a former

schoolhouse that adjoined the church and was bought by Nelson in 1921.

After Opal died, the house fell into disrepair, the taxes weren't paid and Van Buren County put it up for sale to reclaim the tax loss.

When it discovered the treasure, the church advertised the find, as required by law, and the heirs made their claim. They contended the money was "newly discovered property." The matter went to court.

Van Buren County District Judge James Jenkins ruled that Nelson was the owner, but because the treasure was discovered more than five years after Opal's estate was closed the money belonged to the church.

The Supreme Court disagreed and reversed the lower court. "This is type of property to which the true owner retains ownership as against the finder or the owner of the property where it is found," the court said.

Nelson's money wasn't mislaid or abandoned property because "the fact that it was buried in jars and tin cans indicates that the owner was attempting to preserve it," the court said. It wasn't a "treasure trove" that could be kept by whoever found it, as the lower court ruled, and it wasn't "property which had become part of the natural earth" like a meteorite or an ancient sunken boat.

"This is a circumstance which allows reopening of that estate for purposes of administering these assets and making distribution," the court said.

Detlie said the value of the treasure may be greater than $25,000 because it contains several silver dollars and other rare coins and bills.

He said the heirs and the church had agreed amiably to test the issue in court.

The church, however, won't leave empty-handed, he said. It will get a finder's fee amounting to 10 percent of the treasure, and Opal Nelson had willed the church about 20 per cent of her estate.

Treasure may be anywhere! Take a look at the following posted by the Treasurer for the State of Iowa:

The Great Iowa Treasure Hunt
Michael L. Fitzgerald - Iowa Treasurer of State

Iowa Unclaimed Money

Welcome to the Great Iowa Treasure Hunt! Each year millions of dollars are turned over to the state treasury office as lost or abandoned. The property can be from dormant accounts in financial institutions, insurance companies, trust holdings and utility companies.

In addition to money and securities, holdings from safe deposit boxes include such things as watches, jewelry, coins, currency, stamps, historical items and other miscellaneous articles.

Each year billions of dollars in dormant or lost accounts go without ever being

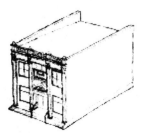

found when governments, companies and banks lose track of the true owner of the money.

This could be due to a host of reasons like marriage break up, misspelled names, businesses going bankrupt, banks getting dissolved, unexpected migration or relocation of jobs, address changes without prior notification, death, post office errors etc. If you know anyone who has ever moved or died, the state of Iowa is probably holding unclaimed funds in their name.

There is an alphabetical list of people whose last known address was in Iowa and who are due to receive money for unclaimed property for the number of years prescribed by statute. The Unclaimed divisions have held the accounts for more than 2 years. Even if your name is not on the list, you may wish to call the Unclaimed Property Division to check if any funds are being held in your name. It is important to note that accounts held less than 2 years are not available for public inspection. Please try using various combinations of your name in order to search for unclaimed money. Also bear in mind that there may be assets in your maiden name.

Iowa unclaimed property or money could be in the form of funds from a dormant checking and savings accounts, un-cashed money orders, cashiers checks, mineral royalty payments, safe deposit box contents, unused gift certificates, unclaimed insurance benefits, lost cash dividends,

stock,  found utility deposits, unclaimed security deposits, and court deposits. Iowa unclaimed property, which was held by another state or a company, is kept in protective custody if they could not be paid to the rightful owner. The owners last recorded state address is always taken into consideration with reference to Iowa's unclaimed money. ·

Make sure you check with every state in which you have ever lived (unclaimed property is generally turned over to the state of your last address as reflected in the records of the business holding your found money, stock, etc.).

In other states, abandoned money is usually held by the State Comptroller's office. Many of them maintain web sites you can check for unclaimed funds.

Do not assume that the business has your last known address. If the business holding your property doesn't have a valid address for you, the property is supposed to be sent to the state where the business was incorporated. Many large corporations are from: Delaware, New Jersey, New York, Iowa, California or other areas.

CHAPTER SIX

PRESERVING OLD MONEY

If you have hidden old money, it's important to know how burying it or hiding it in an attic can affect it. Copper coins can corrode. Silver coins can be attacked by "slime" if stored in old vinyl holders (Many plastic bags and holders contain polyvinyl chlorides that don't mix well with coins).

U.S. Dime That's Turned Green and Slimy From
Being In A Vinyl Coin Holder

Brown manila envelopes contain sulfur that will tarnish coins.

Paper money can rot. The same company, Crane and Company, has made the special type of paper used to make money since 1879. Although a secret, the paper is thought to contain about 25% linen, nylon threads, and 75% cotton. Maybe that's why it won't tear if you leave some money in your washing machine, but since it has linen and cotton fibers, it can be affected by poor storage and deteriorate (just like any other cloth item). I know this from personal experience.

A person brought wads of old currency they had found in cans in a basement into our coin shop. The basement was wet all the time and the notes were damp and moldy. It smelled horrible; it actually took us two days to air out the shop.

There are five primary issues that all hoarders and collectors of old money should be concerned with—acid, relative humidity, temperature, pests, and light.

Acid

Acidic conditions can lead to all sorts of degradation and embrittlement. Acid may be found in certain materials inherent in paper money and also in materials with which paper money and coins comes in contact. Sizes, inks and dyes, bleaches, and impure raw materials can all impact the acidity of paper money.

Wood, cardboard, unstable plastics (including older vinyl coin and currency holders), adhesives, and other acidic papers can come in contact with paper money and coins and transfer their acid.

You can even transfer acid from your hands. A variety of polluting gases, such as oxides of nitrogen from car exhaust, can also increase a paper's acidity.

Relative Humidity

Relative humidity, or RH, is the amount of water vapor in a volume of air, expressed as a percentage of the maximum amount of water vapor the air could hold at a given temperature. Put simply, RH represents the amount of moisture in the air. Paper is a hydroscopic material, which means it has some moisture content under normal circumstances.

When moisture content is too low, paper becomes brittle. High moisture content can cause the growth of molds and start the corrosion of the surfaces of a coin. Coins may actually corrode to the point they're valueless to collectors.

BADLY CORRODED 1857 FLYING EAGLE CENT

Temperature

Temperature and relative humidity are closely related. Changes in temperature cause changes in RH. A rise in temperature usually causes a decrease in RH and vice versa. Stated another way, when it gets hot, the air often gets dry. A combination of high temperatures and low RH can cause paper money to become yellow and brittle. High temperatures can also speed up chemical reactions—some of which are harmful to paper money. Changes in temperature from high to low can cause condensation on the surface of paper, leading to warping, staining and mold formation.

Pests

Mold spores are extremely common and will grow in and on nearly everything if given the opportunity. The molds commonly associated with paper usually only grow when relative humidity is above 70%.

Molds destroy paper's cellulose and sizing, increase acidity, and in some cases leave a variety of colorful stains.

There are a variety of insects that enjoy eating paper money. Most of these bugs prefer still, damp, dark conditions, such as those found in many hiding places. It is very common to find buried or hidden paper money that has been significantly destroyed by hungry insects.

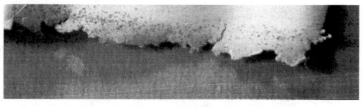

INSECT DAMAGED PAPER

Light

Prolonged and/or intense light exposure can lead to fading and discoloration, and it can cause paper money to become very brittle. Light actually acts in conjunction with oxygen, moisture and pollutants in the air to break up the cellulose structure of paper.

Obviously, the best solution to the above is to hide money in places where damage may be minimized. Avoid damp basements and dry attics to begin with. Put old money in sealable plastic containers. Put a bead of silicone or plastic caulking around the edges.

One individual put gold coins in a PVC plastic pipe, which was O.K. except that he GLUED the caps on the end of the pipe. His widow sawed into the pipe to get the coins out and damaged several in the process.

If you have to bury money, again, use plastic (not paper) containers and seal them tightly. Putting one container inside another works well and gives added protection.

It's wise to check the condition of old money from time to time, even if it's stored in a safety deposit box. Many of the banks in our area are along the river. Some of them have their vaults and safety deposit boxes in the basement.

Old money can become moldy in these places. I recommend airing out your safety deposit boxes from time to time. I also suggest using Silica Gel.

Silica Gel, in many forms, has been the desiccant (drying agent) of choice by government and industry since W.W.II. By surface adsorption, Silica Gel drinks up excess humidity from the air. It prevents condensation within enclosed areas (such as bank boxes) that causes irreparable damage, such as rust, corrosion, tarnish, oxidation, mildew, fungus, mold, odor, spoilage, spotting, toning and stains.

Used within enclosed storage areas, Silica Gel, "drinks up" moisture to create a protective shield of dry air.

Silica Gel is available in Kraft or Tyvek bags or cartons in a variety of sizes. A 2-gram package will protect an area of 12.2 cubic inches. You can go on line to find Silica Gel or your local coin dealer should be able to get it for you.

Individual coins, paper money and rolls of coins can be stored in non-PVC holders. The following illustrates the most popular holders for coins:

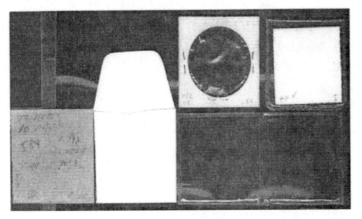

From left to right above: Envelopes, 2x2, flip.

2x2s consist of white cardboard with clear Mylar pocket to allow viewing of coin from both sides. You can describe the coins on the cardboard with pen or pencil. They are called 2x2s because the holder's dimensions measure 2 inches by 2 inches, though most coin holders are this size as well. (In Europe larger sizes are available along with plastic shells into which you place the cardboard holder.)

Paper dust from cardboard can cause spotting over time, though some holders advertise that they're dust free. Staples on staple-types can scratch coins if you're not careful when removing them. Glue on glue-type 2x2s may damage coins over time. 2X2's are somewhat chintzy looking but inexpensive and relatively safe.

Safety flips are an all-plastic two-part holder -- you flip up the part holding the coin to view the coin's reverse. You can choose flips with one pocket (for one coin) or two pockets (for the coin and for the paper insert on which you describe the coin). They're called "safety flips" because they're safe for long-term coin storage.

Plastic Coin Tubes

Safe plastic tubes with screw tops for rolls of coins (they come in different sizes for different kinds of coins) and non-PVC plastic sleeves for paper money are other kinds of safe containers.

In addition to making sure old money is stored safely, there are other things you can do. If you know a relative has hidden money and something happens to them, it's important to take steps immediately to protect not only their hidden money, but their other assets, as well.

I would recommend the following:

1. Change the locks that give access to the home; you don't always know who has keys.

2. Be wary of individuals that can't wait to get inside the home. I don't mean to offend anyone, but this should include attorneys, family members and insurance agents. A lady I once met said she came home for her father's funeral and later found his attorney inside the home. He had not been invited and had no reason to be there. He had no explanation, either, as to why he was there.

3. If anyone comes to the home for any reason, try to be there and make sure they stay focused on why they're there. Don't allow unwanted snooping. If it's a rug cleaning service, they shouldn't be going

through dresser drawers.

4. If items are donated to charity or being thrown out, try to separate them from the rest of the household items. Again, be there when the items are collected.

A lady handling her mother's estate was present when volunteers from a charity came to take items her mother wanted to donate. She vaguely told them the items were in the dining room. The volunteers thought that meant everything in the dining room. Fortunately, she came back into the dining room as a volunteer was removing an 18th century painting from the wall and was about to carry it outside.

The volunteer wasn't intentionally doing anything wrong.

But if she hadn't been there, the painting would have left on the truck with the other donations.

Some final advice:

1. Avoid storing coins and collectibles in cedar chest or cedar closets. The cedar oils will damage the items over time.

2. Educate family members who may inherit thing as to their value and history. Leave notes with valuable items.

3. Never, ever clean old coins and paper money. **The first rule** of coin cleaning is: If you don't know its value, don't clean it, or if you think it is valuable, don't clean it, or if you know it is valuable, don't clean it.

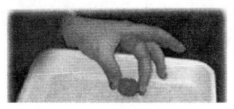

In other words, do not clean your discovered coins; leave them untouched and stored in proper holders. The reason for this is that coin dealers and collectors are interested in purchasing coins in their original condition and natural state of preservation. For example, never clean coins with commercial jewelry and metal polishes or silver tarnish remover, which will remove the toning that normally collects over time on copper and silver coins. Removing tarnish often harms coins, leaving small spots, scratches, or pockmarks that can significantly diminish their numismatic value by up to 90 percent!

ORIGINAL COIN ON TOP; CLEANED COIN ON THE BOTTOM

Chapter Seven

Selling Old Money

If you find old money, or have it hidden somewhere and decide to sell it, it's important to try to have some idea of its value before you talk to anyone about buying it. As I've said throughout this book, there are ways to identify what you have. Local libraries are a good place to start. The Internet has thousands of sights about old coins and currency. Some of my favorite Internet sites are:

The American Numismatic Association at ana@money.org. The ANA is the coin hobby's premier organization for collectors, dealers or anyone interested in old money.

The United States Department of the Treasury at www.ustreas.gov/. There are numerous sites to explore, including Currency & Coins and For The Kids!

The United States Mint at www.usmint.gov/. Check out their Coin of the Month page. You can also buy products on line.

The Bureau of Printing and Engraving at www.bep.treas.gov/. This site has lots of information about U.S. currency. They also have a store where you can buy unusual bank notes.

The Federal Reserve Bank of Richmond at www.richmondfed.org/. Spend time exploring the Money Museum; I think it has one of the easiest to understand and most informative sites for US money.

The British Museum: World of Money at www.thebritishmuseum.ac.uk/. This site offers interesting information about the earliest forms of money, how money is made, etc.

If you can't find something, or if you have an overwhelming amount of material, an appraisal is probably the next best step. Ask your bank for the name of someone they use to appraise old money. Or look up you local coin dealers.

The ANA may be able to help you find someone, too (it's always a good idea to find out what professional organizations a dealer belongs to; if they're a member of the ANA they are supposed to abide by a Code of

Ethics).  The ANA also maintains the Consumer Alert Resources program to help make the coin industry safe for dealers, collectors and investors. The C.A.R.E. program has fraud alerts, educational resources and more to help you.

Whenever possible, it's a good idea to get two or more appraisals, especially if you have a very large collection. Be aware that a dealer or appraiser may charge for the appraisal. Fees can vary widely.

Don't be in a hurry to sell. **There are many ways of selling coins and old paper money. Obviously, one way is to sell to a dealer.** What he or she pays depends upon a lot of factors, including:

1. How easy it will be to resell the material. If a collection has a lot of common, low-grade coins in it that may take time for the dealer to sell, they won't offer you as much as opposed to a collection with much nicer material.
   I still have rolls of common date wheat pennies, partial date Buffalo nickel rolls and other "stuff" lying around that I purchased years ago.

   It's inventory that I accumulated in the process of buying collections; someday I'll sell it but no

   one's knocking on the door looking for it

2. How familiar the dealer may be with the coins or currency. Every dealer has an area that he or she specializes in. They might like old silver

dollars and not have much interest in cents and nickels.

Material that is unfamiliar to them will be approached cautiously. I recall years ago being offered a large collection of British coins. Many of them dated back to medieval times

through the Victorian era.
My first reaction was to run from buying the collection but I did my research and talked to dealers who were more acquainted with this type of material than I was. The end result was I did buy the collection for a price that was fair to everyone.

3. How much cash the dealer can lay his or her hands on. If it's a collection that requires a large amount of money to purchase it, the dealer may be more than a little reluctant to take the risk of buying it and going into debt or wiping out the cash they have on hand.

That's why it's a good idea to get two appraisals. A dealer might pull back a little bit from what he or she should pay for the collection simply because they don't have the resources to buy it or because they're afraid of burying themselves in it.

If it's a large deal, it may take some extra time to pull it all together. Dealers are generally honest people and will tell you up front what they can and can't do.

Please remember that a coin dealer is a businessman or woman just like anyone else. Maybe because it's not an industry people see every day explains why people

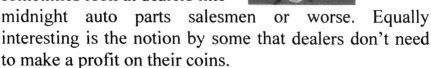

sometimes look at dealers like midnight auto parts salesmen or worse. Equally interesting is the notion by some that dealers don't need to make a profit on their coins.

I once dealt with an older gentleman who had a nice collection of coins he had acquired over the years. He subscribed to the Coin Dealer Newsletter, an industry guide that provides coin prices on a weekly basis. He could look at the Guide and see what "bid" and "ask" prices were for each of his coins.

The "bid" price is a guide to the prices dealers are willing to pay for an average coin of that grade, while the "ask" price is a guide to the prices dealers are asking for an average coin of that grade. Typically there is a minimum 20 percent "spread," or dealer markup, between "bid" and "ask." It is important to keep in mind that these are dealer-to-dealer prices. There is no guarantee that an individual or dealer will be able to find anyone willing to pay the published prices.

He insisted that he needed the "ask" price for his coins, which meant I would have to resell them at or above retail. It didn't leave me much "wiggle" room. If I couldn't get full retail or close to it for a coin, I was stuck with it. He appeared offended when I declined the opportunity to buy his coins.

I have also dealt with other individuals that generously informed me they would buy certain kinds of material from me as long as it was at dealer prices. They weren't a dealer themselves and somehow my not making a nickel on the deal seemed to be something that was expected. My response was if they went to a grocery store or hardware store, did they make them the same kind of offer and how many times were they successful?

Once you agree on a price to purchase your material, you should have no qualms about accepting a business check as payment if you've checked out the dealer and feel comfortable with them. You can also ask for a cashiers check as payment or ask your banker to verify the purchaser has the funds in their account and the checks good. Think about asking for cash.

To start with, very few dealers want to make purchases in cash anymore, especially if a large amount of cash is involved. If payment is made by cash greater than $10,000, it becomes a reportable cash transaction.

Regarding cash transactions, Official General Instructions for IRS Form 8300 read: "Who Must File. - Each person engaged in a trade or business who, during that trade or business, receives more than $10,000 in cash in one transaction or two or more related transactions must file Form 8300. Any transactions conducted between a payer (or its agent) and the recipient in a 24-hour period are related

transactions. This regulation applies to cash - greenbacks, paper money. It does not apply to personal checks, wire transfers, or money market withdrawals. When cashier's checks or money orders are involved, cash reporting may be triggered.

Form 8300's General Instructions define as cash "a cashier's check, bank draft, traveler's check, or money order having a face amount of not more than $10,000."

Using a cashier's check less than $10,000 would be a "cash transaction," but it would not be reportable because it is less than $10,000. However, two cashier's checks, each less than $10,000 but totaling more than $10,000 for a single purchase, would be considered cash and subject to reporting.

Dealers don't want to look like drug dealers or money launderers. Handling a lot of cash may invite trouble. For everyone's safety and peace of mind, it's best to avoid cash transactions.

An auction might be another way to sell old money. **AUCTION TODAY** Auctions can be a good way to sell certain kinds of material, such as rare currency through an auction house that specializes in collectible paper money.

However, if you have a bunch of common date, low-grade silver dollars that are generally worth only six to ten dollars each, an auction might be a bad idea. Your silver dollars may bring a couple of dollars more apiece than what a dealer would pay but the auction fees may be as high as 25% plus there is typically no guarantee that your silver dollars will bring even what the dealer would pay.

Before you consign your coins to an auction, make sure you understand what the fees will be. Also, is advertising included in the auctioneer's fee or is that extra? I have known some very surprised people who thought all they were paying was a straight, say, 20% but were also charged for a portion of the advertising, building rental, security, etc., etc. (what usually happens is the auctioneer counts up the number of consigners and divides these other expenses equally

between them).

Auctioneers for the most part are hard working, honest individuals. You can easily check them out by talking to antique dealers in your area or ask your bank who they use when they need an auctioneer. Auctioneers may also belong to professional organizations such as the National Auctioneers Association or the National Association of Realtors.

The third and final method of selling your coins is consigning them to a coin dealer or broker. The following is an excerpt from an excellent article from Certified Mint, Inc.-www.cmi-gold-silver.com.)::)):

"Consigning coins to a dealer can be productive for all concerned. This is especially true now that third party grading is prevalent and dealer profit margins are generally much smaller than they used to be.

How are consigning coins to a dealer different from consigning the same pieces to an auction?

The most important difference is that you, the seller, know in advance what the sale price will be. Rather than take up too much space, I'll just run through a few points you might consider before consigning coins to a dealer.

1. Always agree on a firm selling price in advance. If you allow the dealer to sell the coins for whatever they can get, chances are you will get less than you expected!

I once gave a nice group of World coins to a dealer who was traveling to Europe. I told him, "Just give it your best shot." I got an overseas call. He told me the market was softening fast. We had better dump the stuff. I told him to go ahead, a small loss was better than a big one. He sold the coins. Yes, you are right again. He sold half of the deal and kept the other half for himself.

He just couldn't bear to part with all the coins in such a strong up market. As with any other type of business, it is better not to give anyone too much rope, they may end up hanging you with it!

2. Only consign coins to a dealer you can trust to pay for the coins when they are sold. The best way to learn to trust a dealer is to test them. Consign just a few coins and see how it goes before turning over

a substantial collection.

3. Decide exactly on what the dealer's consignment fees will be and don't overlook small details. Are you going to be obliged to pay a portion of the advertising costs? Who will pay the postage and insurance charges? Who is responsible should the

dealer be stuck with a bad check or become the victim of credit card fraud and your coins are involved? Are your coins insured while in the dealer's possession? Most dealers, who actively accept consignments from collectors and investors, like to keep things simple.

4. Set an absolute settlement date at which time all coins are paid for, in full, or returned. I don't know why, but a previous customer decided to give another dealer a couple of average condition gold type sets to sell. It took forever for the customer to get paid! First the coins had to be advertised. Then the buyer's checks had to clear. Then the coins had to be shipped. The transaction dragged on. Actually, the dealer had immediately wholesaled the sets and had been paid, but he used every excuse in the book to "borrow", interest free, the consignor's money for as long as he could.

5. Many coins are not worth consigning! Why would either a dealer or a customer bother with a consignment arrangement including a coin that could easily be sold for $95 when the best possible price they could expect to get might be $100? **I would suggest you always get firm cash offers and consider them well before deciding to go the consignment route.**

6. Unless they are quick sellers, don't consign coins that are duplicates of what the dealer already has in stock. Given a choice, I think most dealers would

prefer to sell what they already own rather than a consigned piece.

7. Don't expect a dealer to accept a consignment of coins he will be obliged to sell at inflated prices. If my usual selling price for a coin is $100 don't expect me to try and sell yours for $125, nor should it be offered for just $90. Most dealers are as concerned about treating the buying customer fairly as they are doing a good job for the consignor.

8. Seriously consider sending raw coins to a grading service prior to consigning them. A dealer should be able to review your coins and suggest which ones might be sold for higher prices if they were first graded. It never makes sense to submit coins for grading unless the results will predictably more than offset the grading fees."

However you decide to sell your coins, I hope it is a good experience for you. I have certainly have had some interesting experiences buying and selling coins over the past fifteen years-some good; some not so good. Among them:

❖ I looked at some coins in a basement that had an inch or two of water on the floor. The coins were spread out on a workbench. As I was looking around, I noticed that there was a lot of bad wiring, including an extension cord that was repaired in many places running from an electric box, across the basement floor and then upstairs through a hole in the floor above my head. I gingerly stepped out of the water I was standing in

 and suggested looking at the coins in better light upstairs.

❖ I also buy military collectibles and old guns. I was visiting with a very nice lady who said she wanted to show me a gun her husband had. She went and got it and came back in the room, pointing a huge pistol directly at me! She was a bit unsteady and the pistol was jumping around in her hands. I asked her if it was loaded; she said, "Oh, no, no . . ."

I took it from her. It was a .45 caliber pistol and it was fully loaded, including one in the chamber. The safety was off.

❖ I examined some rolls of silver quarters a lady in her nineties was interested in selling. I checked the rolls to make sure the coins were silver; not clad or junk. As I recall, there were about sixty rolls or $600.00 in face. I offered her 3 times the face value, based on the price of silver at that time. She said she would think about it.

She called a week or so later and said she would sell them to me. I paid for them and took them to a coin show. I offered them to a dealer I have sold silver to many times in the past.

He had a coin counter at the show. He

opened a couple of rolls and dumped them in. The two coins on the ends of the rolls were silver; everything in between was clad, meaning the silver coins had been taken out of the rolls and modern coins, worth face only, had been substituted.

Remarkably, every roll was the same. There was nothing I could do, but I did call the lady when I got home. She didn't know how that could have happened.

❖ I received a call from a lady who wanted to know what a jar of old pennies was worth. I told her I would have to look at them, but suggested that if they were post-1940's wheat pennies, they were worth only .01 to .02 cents, each. She said they were bigger than wheat pennies. After trying to figure out what they were by phone, I offered to go to her home and look at them.

The pennies were modern Eisenhower dollars; I don't know how she confused them with small cents. I was about to leave when she said, "Just a minute . . ." She disappeared and came back with a handful of old cosmetic jars. The jars were stuffed with everything from 18th century silver coins to gold pieces to 1930's tax tokens.

Every time I thought I was done, she would find another jar or cigar box or old purse that had money in it. I ended up buying a lot of nice coins. She had no idea any of it was worth anything. Various family members had saved things over the years and she never tried to find out their value until she called me.

And a final suggestion from me:

- ❑ Never buy corroded, damaged or repaired coins, unless they're a very rare date or there are only a few known specimens.
- ❑ Buy the best grade you can afford. Don't waste money on accumulating a lot of low-end junk coins, unless you are only buying them for their precious metals content.

In summary, I hope this book has been helpful. Possessing old money has attractions that can't always be explained. Whether you are a hoarder or collector or someone who finds a treasure trove, I'm sure the experience will be rewarding and ultimately profitable if you "read the book" and take your time.

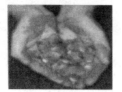

To Order Copies

Please send me _____ copies of
Where Did Grandpa Hide His Money?
at $8.95 each plus $2.00 S/H.
(Make checks payable to **QUIXOTE PRESS**.)

Name _____

Street _____

City _____ State _____ Zip _____

Quixote Press
3544 Blakslee Street
Wever IA 52658
1-800-571-2665

To Order Copies

Please send me _____ copies of
Where Did Grandpa Hide His Money?
at $8.95 each plus $2.00 S/H.
(Make checks payable to **QUIXOTE PRESS**.)

Name _____

Street _____

City _____ State _____ Zip _____

Quixote Press
3544 Blakslee Street
Wever IA 52658
1-800-571-2665

Since you have enjoyed this book, perhaps you would be interested in some of these others from QUIXOTE PRESS.

ARKANSAS BOOKS

ARKANSAS' ROADKILL COOKBOOK
      by Bruce Carlson ....paperback $7.95
REVENGE OF ROADKILL
      by Bruce Carlson ....paperback $7.95
LET'S US GO DOWN TO THE RIVER 'N...
      by Various Authors ....paperback $9.95
TALL TALES OF THE MISSISSIPPI RIVER
      by Dan Titus ....paperback $9.95
LOST & BURIED TREASURE OF THE MISSISSIPPI RIVER
      by Netha Bell & Gary Scholl ....paperback $9.95
TALES OF HACKETT'S CREEK
      by Dan Titus ....paperback $9.95
101 WAYS TO USE A DEAD RIVER FLY
      by Bruce Carlson ....paperback $7.95
VACANT LOT, SCHOOL YARD & BACK ALLEY GAMES
      by Various Authors ....paperback $9.95
HOW TO TALK MIDWESTERN
      by Robert Thomas ....paperback $7.95
ARKANSAS COOKIN'
      by Bruce Carlson ....(3x5) paperback $5.95

DAKOTA BOOKS

HOW TO TALK DAKOTA ....paperback $7.95
Some Pretty Tame, but Kinda Funny Stories About Early
DAKOTA LADIES-OF-THE-EVENING
      by Bruce Carlson ....paperback $9.95
SOUTH DAKOTA ROADKILL COOKBOOK
      by Bruce Carlson ....paperback $7.95

REVENGE OF ROADKILL

by Bruce Carlson ....paperback $7.95

101 WAYS TO USE A DEAD RIVER FLY

by Bruce Carlson ....paperback $7.95

LET'S US GO DOWN TO THE RIVER 'N...

by Various Authors ....paperback $9.95

LOST & BURIED TREASURE OF THE MISSOURI RIVER

by Netha Bell ....paperback $9.95

MAKIN' DO IN SOUTH DAKOTA

by Various Authors ....paperback $9.95

THE DAKOTAS' VANSHING OUTHOUSE

by Bruce Carlson ....paperback $9.95

VACANT LOT, SCHOOL YARD & BACK ALLEY GAMES

by Various Authors ....paperback $9.95

HOW TO TALK MIDWESTERN

by Robert Thomas ....paperback $7.95

DAKOTA COOKIN'

by Bruce Carlson ....(3x5) paperback $5.95

ILLINOIS BOOKS

ILLINOIS COOKIN'

by Bruce Carlson ....(3x5) paperback $5.95

THE VANISHING OUTHOUSE OF ILLINOIS

by Bruce Carlson ....paperback $9.95

A FIELD GUIDE TO ILLINOIS' CRITTERS

by Bruce Carlson ....paperback $7.95

Some Pretty Tame, but Kinda Funny Stories About Early
ILLINOIS LADIES-OF-THE-EVENING

by Bruce Carlson ....paperback $9.95

ILLINOIS' ROADKILL COOKBOOK

    by Bruce Carlson ....paperback $7.95

101 WAYS TO USE A DEAD RIVER FLY

    by Bruce Carlson ....paperback $7.95

HOW TO TALK ILLINOIS

    by Netha Bell ....paperback $7.95

TALL TALES OF THE MISSISSIPPI RIVER

    by Dan Titus ....paperback $9.95

TALES OF HACKETT'S CREEK

    by Dan Titus ....paperback $9.95

LOST & BURIED TREASURE OF THE MISSISSIPPI RIVER

    by Netha Bell & Gary Scholl ....paperback $9.95

STRANGE FOLKS ALONG THE MISSISSIPPI

    by Pat Wallace ....paperback $9.95

LET'S US GO DOWN TO THE RIVER 'N...

    by Various Authors ....paperback $9.95

MISSISSIPPI RIVER PO' FOLK

    by Pat Wallace ....paperback $9.95

GHOSTS OF THE MISSISSIPPI RIVER
(from Keokuk to St. Louis)

    by Bruce Carlson ....paperback $9.95

GHOSTS OF THE MISSISSIPPI RIVER
(from Dubuque to Keokuk)

    by Bruce Carlson ....paperback $9.95

MAKIN' DO IN ILLINOIS

    by Various Authors ....paperback $9.95

MY VERY FIRST

    by Various Authors ....paperback $9.95

VACANT LOT, SCHOOL YARD & BACK ALLEY GAMES

    by Various Authors ....paperback $9.95

HOW TO TALK MIDWESTERN

    by Robert Thomas ....paperback $7.95

INDIANA BOOKS

HOW TO TALK HOOSIER
By Netha Bell .paperback $7.95
REVENGE OF ROADKILL
by Bruce Carlson . . . . .paperback $7.95
LET'S US GO DOWN TO THE RIVER 'N...
by Various Authors . . . . .paperback $9.95
101 WAYS TO USE A DEAD RIVER FLY
by Bruce Carlson . . . . .paperback $7.95
VACANT LOT, SCHOOL YARD & BACK ALLEY GAMES
by Various Authors . . . . .paperback $9.95
HOW TO TALK MIDWESTERN
by Robert Thomas . . . . .paperback $7.95
INDIANA PRAIRIE SKIRTS
by Bev Faaborg & Lois Brinkman . . . . .paperback $9.95
INDIANA COOKIN'
by Bruce Carlson . . . .(3x5) paperback $5.95

IOWA BOOKS

IOWA COOKIN'
by Bruce Carlson . . . .(3x5) paperback $5.95
IOWA'S ROADKILL COOKBOOK
by Bruce Carlson . . . . .paperback $7.95
REVENGE OF ROADKILL
by Bruce Carlson . . . . .paperback $7.95
GHOSTS OF THE AMANA COLONIES
by Lori Erickson . . . . .paperback $9.95
GHOSTS OF THE IOWA GREAT LAKES
by Bruce Carlson .paperback $9.95
GHOSTS OF THE MISSISSIPPI RIVER
(from Dubuque to Keokuk)
by Bruce Carlson . . . . .paperback $9.95

GHOSTS OF THE MISSISSIPPI RIVER
(from Minneapolis to Dubuque)
     by Bruce Carlson ....paperback $9.95
GHOSTS OF POLK COUNTY, IOWA
     by Tom Welch ....paperback $9.95
TALES OF HACKETT'S CREEK
     by Dan Titus ....paperback $9.95
TALL TALES OF THE MISSISSIPPI RIVER
     by Dan Titus ....paperback $9.95
101 WAYS TO USE A DEAD RIVER FLY
     by Bruce Carlson ....paperback $7.95
LET'S US GO DOWN TO THE RIVER 'N...
     by Various Authors ....paperback $9.95
TRICKS WE PLAYED IN IOWA
     by Various Authors ....paperback $9.95
IOWA, THE LAND BETWEEN THE VOWELS
(farm boy stories from the early 1900s)
     by Bruce Carlson ....paperback $9.95
LOST & BURIED TREASURE OF THE MISSISSIPPI RIVER
     by Netha Bell & Gary Scholl ....paperback $9.95
Some Pretty Tame, but Kinda Funny Stories About Early
IOWA LADIES-OF-THE-EVENING
     by Bruce Carlson ....paperback $9.95
THE VANISHING OUTHOUSE OF IOWA
     by Bruce Carlson ....paperback $9.95
IOWA'S EARLY HOME REMEDIES
     by 26 Students at Wapello Elem. School ..paperback $9.95
IOWA - A JOURNEY IN A PROMISED LAND
     by Kathy Yoder ....paperback $16.95
LOST & BURIED TREASURE OF THE MISSOURI RIVER
     by Netha Bell ....paperback $9.95
FIELD GUIDE TO IOWA'S CRITTERS
     by Bruce Carlson ....paperback $7.95
OLD IOWA HOUSES, YOUNG LOVES
     by Bruce Carlson ....paperback $9.95

SKUNK RIVER ANTHOLOGY
  by Gene Olson . . . . .paperback $9.95
VACANT LOT, SCHOOL YARD & BACK ALLEY GAMES
  by Various Authors . . . . .paperback $9.95
HOW TO TALK MIDWESTERN
  by Robert Thomas . . . . .paperback $7.95

KANSAS BOOKS

HOW TO TALK KANSAS . . . . .paperback $7.95
STOPOVER IN KANSAS
  by Jon McAlpin . . . . .paperback $9.95
LET'S US GO DOWN TO THE RIVER 'N...
  by Various Authors . . . . .paperback $9.95
LOST & BURIED TREASURE OF THE MISSOURI RIVER
  by Netha Bell .paperback $9.95
101 WAYS TO USE A DEAD RIVER FLY
  by Bruce Carlson . . . . .paperback $7.95
VACANT LOT, SCHOOL YARD & BACK ALLEY GAMES
  by Various Authors . . . . .paperback $9.95
HOW TO TALK MIDWESTERN
  by Robert Thomas . . . . .paperback $7.95

KENTUCKY BOOKS

TALES OF HACKETT'S CREEK
  by Dan Titus . . . . .paperback $9.95
LOST & BURIED TREASURE OF THE MISSISSIPPI RIVER
  by Netha Bell & Gary Scholl . . . . .paperback $9.95
LET'S US GO DOWN TO THE RIVER 'N...
  by Various Authors . . . . .paperback $9.95

101 WAYS TO USE A DEAD RIVER FLY
by Bruce Carlson ....paperback $7.95
TALL TALES OF THE MISSISSIPPI RIVER
by Dan Titus ....paperback $9.95
MY VERY FIRST
by Various Authors ....paperback $9.95
VACANT LOT, SCHOOL YARD & BACK ALLEY GAMES
by Various Authors ....paperback $9.95

MICHIGAN BOOKS

MICHIGAN COOKIN'
by Bruce Carlson ....paperback $7.95
MICHIGAN'S ROADKILL COOKBOOK
by Bruce Carlson ....paperback $7.95
MICHIGAN'S VANISHING OUTHOUSE
by Bruce Carlson ....paperback $9.95

MINNESOTA BOOKS

MINNESOTA'S ROADKILL COOKBOOK
by Bruce Carlson ....paperback $7.95
REVENGE OF ROADKILL
by Bruce Carlson ....paperback $7.95
GHOSTS OF THE MISSISSIPPI RIVER
(from Minneapolis to Dubuque)
by Bruce Carlson ....paperback $9.95
LAKES COUNTRY COOKBOOK
by Bruce Carlson ....paperback $11.95

TALES OF HACKETT'S CREEK
     by Dan Titus . . . . .paperback $9.95
MINNESOTA'S VANISHING OUTHOUSE
     by Bruce Carlson . . . . .paperback $9.95
TALL TALES OF THE MISSISSIPPI RIVER
     by Dan Titus . . . . .paperback $9.95
Some Pretty Tame, but Kinda Funny Stories About Early
MINNESOTA LADIES-OF-THE-EVENING
     by Bruce Carlson . . . . .paperback $9.95
101 WAYS TO USE A DEAD RIVER FLY
     by Bruce Carlson . . . . .paperback $7.95
LOST & BURIED TEASURE OF THE MISSISSIPPI RIVER
     by Netha Bell & Gary Scholl . . . . .paperback $9.95
VACANT LOT, SCHOOL YARD & BACK ALLEY GAMES
     by Various Authors . . . . .paperback $9.95
HOW TO TALK MIDWESTERN
     by Robert Thomas . . . . .paperback $7.95
MINNESOTA COOKIN'
     by Bruce Carlson . . . .(3x5) paperback $5.95

MISSOURI BOOKS

MISSOURI COOKIN'
     by Bruce Carlson . . . .(3x5) paperback $5.95
MISSOURI'S ROADKILL COOKBOOK
     by Bruce Carlson . . . . .paperback $7.95
REVENGE OF THE ROADKILL
     by Bruce Carlson . . . . .paperback $7.95
LET'S US GO DOWN TO THE RIVER 'N...
     by Various Authors . . . . .paperback $9.95

LAKES COUNTRY COOKBOOK

    by Bruce Carlson ....paperback $11.95

101 WAYS TO USE A DEAD RIVER FLY

    by Bruce Carlson ....paperback $7.95

TALL TALES OF THE MISSISSIPPI RIVER

    by Dan Titus ....paperback $9.95

TALES OF HACKETT'S CREEK

    by Dan Titus ....paperback $9.95

STRANGE FOLKS ALONG THE MISSISSIPPI

    by Pat Wallace ....paperback $9.95

LOST AND BURIED TREASURE OF THE MISSOURI RIVER

    by Netha Bell ....paperback $9.95

HOW TO TALK MISSOURIAN

    by Bruce Carlson ....paperback $7.95

VACANT LOT, SCHOOL YARD & BACK ALLEY GAMES

    by Various Authors ....paperback $9.95

HOW TO TALK MIDWESTERN

    by Robert Thomas ....paperback $7.95

LOST & BURIED TREASURE OF THE MISSISSIPPI RIVER

    by Netha Bell & Gary Scholl ....paperback $9.95

MISSISSIPPI RIVER PO' FOLK

    by Pat Wallace ....paperback $9.95

Some Pretty Tame, but Kinda Funny Stories About Early
MISSOURI LADIES-OF-THE-EVENING

    by Bruce Carlson ....paperback $9.95

A FIELD GUIDE TO MISSOURI'S CRITTERS

    by Bruce Carlson ....paperback $7.95

EARLY MISSOURI HOME REMEDIES

    by Various Authors ....paperback $9.95

UNDERGROUND MISSOURI

    by Bruce Carlson ....paperpback $9.95

MISSISSIPPI RIVER COOKIN' BOOK

    by Bruce Carlson ....paperback $11.95

NEBRASKA BOOKS

LOST & BURIED TREASURE OF THE MISSOURI RIVER
        by Netha Bell ....paperback $9.95
101 WAYS TO USE A DEAD RIVER FLY
        by Bruce Carlson ....paperback $7.95
LET'S US GO DOWN TO THE RIVER 'N...
        by Various Authors ....paperback $9.95
HOW TO TALK MIDWESTERN
        by Robert Thomas ....paperback $7.95
VACANT LOT, SCHOOL YARD & BACK ALLEY GAMES
        by Various Authors ....paperback $9.95

TENNESSEE BOOKS

TALES OF HACKETT'S CREEK
        by Dan Titus ....paperback $9.95
TALL TALES OF THE MISSISSIPPI RIVER
        by Dan Titus ....paperback $9.95
UNSOLVED MYSTERIES OF THE MISSISSIPPI
        by Netha Bell ....paperback $9.95
LOST & BURIED TREASURE OF THE MISSISSIPPI RIVER
        by Netha Bell & Gary Scholl ....paperback $9.95
LET'S US GO DOWN TO THE RIVER 'N...
        by Various Authors ....paperback $9.95
101 WAYS TO USE A DEAD RIVER FLY
        by Bruce Carlson ....paperback $7.95
VACANT LOT, SCHOOL YARD & BACK ALLEY GAMES
        by Various Authors ....paperback $9.95

WISCONSIN

HOW TO TALK WISCONSIN . . . . .paperback $7.95

WISCONSIN COOKIN'
by Bruce Carlson . . . .(3x5) paperback $5.95

WISCONSIN'S ROADKILL COOKBOOK
by Bruce Carlson . . . . .paperback $7.95

REVENGE OF ROADKILL
by Bruce Carlson . . . . .paperback $7.95

TALL TALES OF THE MISSISSIPPI RIVER
by Dan Titus . . . . .paperback $9.95

LAKES COUNTRY COOKBOOK
by Bruce Carlson . . . . .paperback $11.95

TALES OF HACKETT'S CREEK
by Dan Titus . . . . .paperback $9.95

LET'S US GO DOWN TO THE RIVER 'N...
by Various Authors . . . . .paperback $9.95

101 WAYS TO USE A DEAD RIVER FLY
by Bruce Carlson . . . . .paperback $7.95

LOST & BURIED TREASURE OF THE MISSISSIPPI RIVER
by Netha Bell & Gary Scholl . . . . .paperback $9.95

HOW TO TALK MIDWESTERN
by Robert Thomas . . . . .paperback $7.95

VACANT LOT, SCHOOL YARD & BACK ALLEY GAMES
by Various Authors . . . . .paperback $9.95

MY VERY FIRST
by Various Authors . . . . .paperback $9.95

EARLY WISCONSIN HOME REMEDIES
by Various Authors . . . . .paperback $9.95

THE VANISHING OUTHOUSE OF WISCONSIN
by Bruce Carlson . . . . .paperback $9.95

GHOSTS OF DOOR COUNTY, WISCONSIN
by Geri Rider .paperback $9.95

RIVER BOOKS

ON THE SHOULDERS OF A GIANT
      by M. Cody and D. Walker . . . . .paperback $9.95
SKUNK RIVER ANTHOLOGY
      by Gene "Will" Olson . . . . .paperback $9.95
JACK KING vs DETECTIVE MACKENZIE
      by Netha Bell .paperback $9.95
LOST & BURIED TREASURE OF THE MISSISSIPPI RIVER
      by Netha Bell & Gary Scholl . . . . .paperback $9.95
MISSISSIPPI RIVER PO' FOLK
      by Pat Wallace . . . . .paperback $9.95
STRANGE FOLKS ALONG THE MISSISSIPPI
      by Pat Wallace . . . . .paperback $9.95
TALES OF HACKETT'S CREEK
(1940s Mississippi River kids)
      by Dan Titus . . . . .paperback $9.95
101 WAYS TO USE A DEAD RIVER FLY
      by Bruce Carlson . . . . .paperback $7.95
LET'S US GO DOWN TO THE RIVER 'N...
      by Various Authors . . . . .paperback $9.95
LOST & BURIED TREASURE OF THE MISSOURI
      by Netha Bell .paperback $9.95
LIL' RED BOOK OF FISHING TIPS
      by Tom Hollatz . . . . .paperback $7.95

COOKBOOKS

THE BACK-TO-THE SUPPER TABLE COOKBOOK
      by Susie Babbington . . . . .paperback $11.95
THE COVERED BRIDGES COOKBOOK
      by Bruce Carlson . . . . .paperback $11.95
COUNTRY COOKING-RECIPES OF MY AMISH HERITAGE
      by Kathy Yoder . . . . .paperback $9.95
CIVIL WAR COOKIN', STORIES, 'N SUCH
      by Darlene Funkhouser . . . . .paperback $9.95

SOUTHERN HOMEMADE
by Lorraine Lott . . . . .paperback $11.95
THE ORCHARD, BERRY PATCHES, AND GARDEN CKBK
by Bruce Carlson . . . . .paperback $11.95
THE BODY SHOP COOKBOOK
by Sherrill Wolff . . . . .paperback $14.95
CAMP COOKING COOKBOOK
by Mary Ann Kerl . . . . .paperback $9.95
FARMERS' MARKET COOKBOOK
by Bruce Carlson . . . . .paperback $9.95
HERBAL COOKERY
by Dixie Stephen . . . . .paperback $9.95
MAD ABOUT GARLIC
by Pat Reppert . . . . .paperback $9.95
BREADS! BREADS! BREADS!
by Mary Ann Kerl . . . . .paperback $9.95
PUMPKIN PATCHES, PROVERBS & PIES
by Cherie Reilly . . . . .paperback $9.95
ARIZONA COOKING
by Barbara Soden . . . . .paperback $5.95
SOUTHWEST COOKING
by Barbara Soden . . . . .paperback $5.95
EATIN' OHIO
by Rus Pishnery . . . . .paperback $9.95
EATIN' ILLINOIS
by Rus Pishnery . . . . .paperback $9.95
KENTUCKY COOKIN'
by Marilyn Tucker Carlson . . . . .paperback $5.95
INDIANA COOKIN'
by Bruce Carlson . . . . .paperback $5.95
KANSAS COOKIN'
by Bruce Carlson . . . . .paperback $5.95

NEW JERSEY COOKING

    by Bruce Carlson ....paperback $5.95

NEW MEXICO COOKING

    by Barbara Soden ....paperback $5.95

NEW YORK COOKIN'

    by Bruce Carlson ....paperback $5.95

OHIO COOKIN'

    by Bruce Carlson ....paperback $5.95

PENNSYLVANIA COOKING

    by Bruce Carlson ....paperback $5.95

AMISH-MENNONITE STRAWBERRY COOKBOOK

    by Alta Kauffman ....paperback $5.95

APPLES! APPLES! APPLES!

    by Melissa Mosley ....paperback $5.95

APPLES GALORE!!!

    by Bruce Carlson ....paperback $5.95

BERRIES! BERRIES! BERRIES!

    by Melissa Mosley ....paperback $5.95

BERRIES GALORE!!!

    by Bruce Carlson ....paperback $5.95

CHERRIES! CHERRIES! CHERRIES!

    by Marilyn Carlson ....paperback $5.95

CITRUS! CITRUS! CITRUS!

    by Lisa Nafziger ....paperback $5.95

COOKING WITH CIDER

    by Bruce Carlson ....paperback $5.95

COOKING WITH THINGS THAT GO BAA

    by Bruce Carlson ....paperback $5.95

COOKING WITH THINGS THAT GO CLUCK

    by Bruce Carlson ....paperback $5.95

COOKING WITH THINGS THAT GO MOO

    by Bruce Carlson ....paperback $5.95

COOKING WITH THINGS THAT GO OINK

    by Bruce Carlson ....paperback $5.95

GARLIC! GARLIC! GARLIC!
  by Bruce Carlson ....paperback $5.95
KID COOKIN'
  by Bev Faaborg ....paperback $5.95
THE KID'S GARDEN FUN BOOK
  by Theresa McKeown ....paperback $5.95
KID'S PUMPKIN FUN BOOK
  by J. Ballhagen ....paperback $5.95
NUTS! NUTS! NUTS!
  by Melissa Mosley ....paperback $5.95
PEACHES! PEACHES! PEACHES!
  by Melissa Mosley ....paperback $5.95
PUMPKINS! PUMPKINS! PUMPKINS!
  by Melissa Mosley ....paperback $5.95
VEGGIE-FRUIT-NUT MUFFIN RECIPES
  by Darlene Funkhouser ....paperback $5.95
WORKING GIRL COOKING
  by Bruce Carlson ....paperback $5.95
SOME LIKE IT HOT!!!
  by Barbara Soden ....paperback $5.95
HOW TO COOK SALSA
  by Barbara Soden ....paperback $5.95
COOKING WITH FRESH HERBS
  by Eleanor Wagner ....paperback $5.95
BUFFALO COOKING
  by Momfeather ....paperback $5.95
NO STOVE-NO SHARP KNIFE KIDS NO-COOK COOKBOOK
  by Timmy Denning ....paperback $9.95

MISCELLANEOUS

HALLOWEEN
  by Bruce Carlson ....paperback $9.95
VEGGIE TALK
  by Glynn Singleton ....paperback $6.95
WASHASHORE
  by Margaret Potter ....paperback $9.95
PRINCES AND TOADS
  by Dr. Sharon Tobler ....paperback $12.95
HOW SOON CAN YOU GET HERE, DOC?
  by David Wynia, DVM ....paperback $9.95
MY PAW WAS A GREAT DANE
  by R. E. Rasmussen, DVM ....paperback $14.95

To order any of these books
from Quixote Press
call
1-800-571-2665